Wired for Culture

How E-mail is Revolutionizing Arts Marketing

Eugene Carr

PATRON PUBLISHING
NEW YORK

Patron Publishing
A division of Patron Technology, LLC
850 Seventh Avenue, Suite 704
New York, NY 10019

Cover and text design by Jonathan Gullery

Library of Congress Control Number: 2003104484

ISBN: 0-9729141-0-2

First Printing April 2003

Printed in the United States of America

Dedication

This book is dedicated to the thousands of under-appreciated arts marketers struggling against all odds to build audiences for the future.

Acknowledgements

Michelle Kettner was the project manager for this book and deserves credit for turning it into a reality with lightning fast speed.

In addition, the following people's advice, contributions, encouragement and positive spirit helped make this book possible. I offer my thanks and appreciation.

Jane Chafin, Patron Technology
Larry Schwartz, NewNetCo
Mark Famiglietti, NewNetCo
Betsy Jacks, Whitney Museum of American Art
Jim Hirsch, CAPA Chicago
Dan McMahon, Goodspeed Musicals
Janice Chaikelson, The New Victory Theater
Judith Ribbler, Searchline Associates
David Berkowitz, eMarketer

Contents

CHAPTER 1

Introduction

Who is this book for, and why should you read it?

Fellow arts marketers, there's a new and fantastic world of e-mail marketing waiting at your fingertips. It's faster, cheaper and more effective than practically any other kind of marketing, and arts patrons are responding to it in amazing ways. In this era of budget cutting and last minute ticket buying, e-mail can help you do MORE marketing for LESS money and get BETTER results.

Consider:

- In 2002, Goodspeed Musicals tested e-mail for the first time in its renewal campaign and motivated 47% of those e-mailed to renew online!
- CAPA in Chicago sold $40,000 of tickets to an Ellen DeGeneres concert through its e-mail list of 24,000 names, at a marketing cost of $300.
- The Whitney Museum of American Art now promotes special events using e-mail, reaching out to niche audiences cost-effectively for the first time.

I first recognized the potential for this kind of marketing in 1995 when I was serving as executive director of the American Symphony Orchestra, marketing concerts at Carnegie Hall and Lincoln Center. It seemed to me that a new world of opportunity in reaching arts patrons online was rapidly emerging.

I began working on a nationwide arts information Web site, CultureFinder.com, in the evenings and on weekends. After it won a national competition and received an investment from AOL, I left the orchestra to develop the site full time. One of the first things I did was initiate a weekly e-mail newsletter. Today, the subscriber base of that newsletter is about 50,000.

Much of this book draws on my CultureFinder.com experience as well as more recent work with clients of Patron Technology, a company I founded in 2001. Patron Technology provides the arts industry with affordable, cutting-edge online marketing tools and techniques. Our software service, PatronMail®, is now being used by over 90 arts organizations in the U.S. and the U.K.

As part of this work, I have given dozens of seminars and talks on e-mail marketing at arts industry conferences and meetings. Inevitably someone comes up to me afterwards and says, "Wow, that was great and I'm now totally convinced. However, my boss is the one that needs to understand this and she couldn't be here today. Is there something you can give me in writing that sums this all up?"

This book is for you the arts marketing director, your executive director, a board member, or anyone that isn't convinced that adopting a professional e-mail marketing program is likely to be the single most financially sound marketing investment you'll make in the next year. Even though this book focuses on not-for-profit arts organizations, it's also equally relevant for any for-profit business with a constituency or customer base that would benefit from regular e-mail communications.

My aim is to help you understand the fundamentals of why this kind of marketing works, and to provide basic information about how you can get started utilizing e-mail to revolutionize your marketing efforts.

The first section focuses on online consumer behavior. To properly understand how and why e-mail marketing works, we'll examine how arts consumers currently use the Web and react and respond to e-mail.

I'll use industry data as well as the results of several years of study of CultureFinder.com subscribers' use of the online medium. I'll then focus in on arts patrons' use of e-mail and explain why the potential is so good. We'll look at some real-world results from arts organizations that are doing this kind of cutting-edge marketing today.

My "Smart Tips for E-mail Marketing" provides the nuts and bolts of what you need to do to get started properly. I'll finish with a discussion of how to develop your own online marketing strategy and a selection of frequently asked questions.

With that as a plan, I invite you to open your minds to the new world of e-mail marketing!`

CHAPTER 2

Our E-mail Marketing Future

What's the big opportunity here?

The overall message of this book rests on the premise that the arts patrons you want to reach now live in an online world offering you tremendous new opportunities to reach them more effectively and cost-efficiently than ever before.

A significant and growing portion of arts patrons embraces the Internet as a better way to get information, and prefers e-mail for getting and responding to your marketing messages.

Let's first dispel a widespread misconception: <u>Effective online arts marketing is not all about having a great Web site.</u>

This notion is a leftover from the dot-com hype of the late 1990s. Back then, everyone believed that if you built a "great" Web site (ostensibly one that had changing content, interactive elements and flashy graphics) you'd develop a loyal audience that would return on a regular basis.

While that may be true for sites that deal with information that is both continually changing and critically important to people's lives, it does not apply directly to the arts. Sports, news, weather, health, and financial sites (such as cnn.com, schwab.com, espn.com, webmd.com) tie their success to a large and frequently returning audience.

For the most part, however, arts sites should not aspire to this goal. There's no perception among arts patrons that arts organizations' sites are of critical importance to their lives. Rather, they perceive these sites as mere repositories for schedule and program information. Expecting visitors to remember your Web address and regularly check your site for new information is mostly wishful thinking.

That's why the real action in online arts marketing lies with e-mail.

E-mail is a "push" technology. You push information out to your patrons when you want them to know about it and to respond. You're in control of the marketing dialogue.

Effective e-mail communication can help you build long-term relationships with your patrons in ways that you could not do as efficiently or cost-effectively by any other means.

This is not only important for marketers, but also for development and fundraising executives, whose job is focused on building an emotional bond with patrons that will ultimately translate into voluntary donations.

Finally, e-mail marketing works quickly and is more cost-effective than the most common arts marketing methods: print ads, direct mail, radio or telemarketing.

Since e-mail marketing is really just another form of direct mail, let's briefly compare its benefits with direct mail in print. (We'll analyze this in more detail later.)

- *Lower cost:* You will spend pennies per e-mail, compared with an amount typically ranging from $.50 to $2.50 per piece for direct mail.
- *More accurate reporting and tracking:* Direct mail offers little information beyond purchase rates. E-mail marketing allows you to measure most key aspects of the marketing process, and does so in real time.
- *Faster delivery and quicker response:* About 80% of your response rate will come within the first 48 hours, compared with days to weeks for direct mail.

With this in mind, I urge you to subject all your marketing efforts to a return on investment (ROI) analysis. How much do you invest in each marketing (or fundraising) method, versus how much you get back in dollars or unit transactions?

In these very tough economic times (and even when the economy improves) we must rethink the way we spend scarce marketing dollars. We can't afford to do marketing that seems like a good idea, without really knowing what each and every effort returns. I subscribe to the thinking: *if you can't track it, don't do it.*

When you start thinking this way, you'll quickly learn that e-mail marketing is the most effective marketing medium for the arts. You can achieve spectacular results for relatively little investment and build relationships with your patrons more cost-effectively than ever before.

CHAPTER 3

Consumer Behavior on the Web

How do patrons use the Internet anyway?

To understand why e-mail marketing is such an effective communication tool, we must first come to a basic understanding about consumer behavior on the Web. How consumers use Web sites, or rather don't use them, is our first exploration.

Who exactly is online?

The U.S. online audience now represents about 168 million people. To put this in context, there are 290 million Americans living in the U.S., of which 225 million are over 14 years old.[1]

When I started working in this industry in 1996, only 13% of the population was online, representing about 14 million people.[2] The majority of them were either young and technically adept, or academics.

Today the Internet audience has grown ten-fold and is a mass-market medium. In comparison with the 168 million people online, there were estimated to be 140 million cell phone subscribers in the U.S in 2002,[3] and about 72 million U.S. households with basic cable TV subscriptions in 2001.[4]

The following figure shows that the largest growth of Internet users in this country came between 1996 and 2000. Estimates are that this number will continue to grow modestly over the next couple of years.

Figure 1[5]

Internet Penetration of U.S. Population

Millions of Users	37	60	83	104	122	138	153	168	182	194
Percentage of U.S. Population	14%	22%	31%	38%	44%	50%	56%	60%	64%	68%
Year	1996	1997	1998	1999	2000	2001	2002	2003	2004	2005

Predicting the online arts audience

In comparison with the general public, arts audiences are relatively wealthy. The average household income of CultureFinder.com newsletter subscribers is $75,000. This is about 50% higher than the average U.S. online household income of $49,000.[6]

And, as you'll see here, as income increases so too does the likelihood that people will have Internet access.

Figure 2[7]

Internet Penetration of Internet Access by Household Income

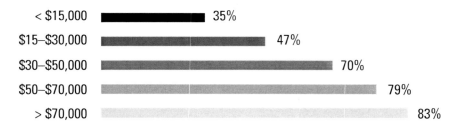

How does the average income of your patron base match up with this figure?

But what about age?

It's also true that traditional arts audiences tend to be older than for other types of entertainment. For decades, studies have covered the subject of the aging of the audience and corresponding implications for the future of the arts. I'll steer clear of that discussion by merely noting that this medium now reaches all age groups.

Figure 3 shows that age ranges up to 55 years old are over 75% connected.

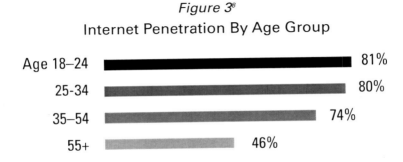

Figure 3[8]
Internet Penetration By Age Group

You may be saying to yourself "I knew there was a catch, this doesn't apply to my organization, because our audience is OLD."

First of all, a meaningful portion, 46%, of those over 55 have Internet access. Even though that's a lower number than younger age segments, keep this percentage in mind when you look out at your audience. At least one of every two of these patrons is online today!

The Internet industry research group IDC forecasts that the over-55 audience will double between the years 2000 and 2005. I'll bet if you pay attention to Internet advertising during the next few years you'll see a lot of it targeted directly to seniors.

Now let's turn to a consideration of how consumers actually use the Web. How do they spend their time online, and what matters most to them?

The Pew Research Center estimates that 87% of Internet users have home Internet access. This compares with about 52% who claim they go online from their workplace. Further, Pew reports that 23% say they at least occasionally go online from other places, such as cyber cafes, libraries or schools.[9]

For those of you familiar with your own site's traffic reports, some of this may be old news. But, it bears repeating since most of the mistakes made by Web developers ignore the basic facts of online behavior.

Fact: Arts patrons are a fickle bunch. They want to look at your Web site, find information and leave as fast as possible. It's nothing personal, but these are busy people.

Let me emphasize that the information they seek is probably available elsewhere – just more slowly. For instance, the time and date of your next performance is surely available by calling the box office, or in a local newspaper or radio ad. However, the Web provides a more convenient way to access this information.

So, if your site doesn't make it <u>faster and easier</u> to find the information they seek, your patron is frustrated. And, once frustrated, a repeat visit is much less likely.

Unfortunately, many sites ignore these obvious facts and are highly complicated, disorganized and confusing. Too many Web developers want to show off "cool" technology rather than provide a simple, clean, clear online experience.

When we examine overall industry statistics about consumer behavior online, we quickly see evidence of this:

Question: What's the average time spent during an online session?

Answer: 31 minutes

Question: What's the average time spent on each page?

Answer: 48 seconds[10]

Now let's look at average visit times for arts sites to further illustrate this point.

	time spent per visit	pages viewed per visit
New York Philharmonic	9 min 14 sec	5.25
Goodspeed Musicals	1 min 48 sec	4.34
The Public Theater	1 min 39 sec	3.0
The Whitney	2 min 40 sec	1.4

Once online, viewers are buyers

Long gone are the days in which the Internet was only about getting information. And long gone are the days when consumers were afraid to enter their credit card information online.

Indeed, online revenues have been growing at a dizzying pace for the last several years.

Figure 4[11]
Online Shopping by Year

$ in billions	$12	$24	$34	$48	$64	$83	$104	$130
Year	1999	2000	2001	2002	2003	2004	2005	2006

Over the 2002 Christmas holiday, Internet sales surpassed $13 billion, representing a 24% increase over the previous year.[12]

This shows in a tangible way that we're now in the middle of a dramatic change in consumer behavior. There's been steady and con-

19

tinuing consumer adoption of online commerce, which has been increasing since the beginning of the online era in the mid-90s. The ups and downs of the dot-com stock market have eclipsed the real story – which is the amazing acceptance of this medium for online commerce.

Even though it's taken a few years to get to this point, the evidence is clear that Internet shopping offers tremendous advantages when done well.

What attracts most consumers' attention?

A review of sites with the largest traffic online reveals something very interesting about consumers' interest in online event information and ticketing. Here is a list of the most frequently visited Web sites in early March, 2003.[13]

Rank	Property	Unique Audience (millions)
3	Yahoo!	40.0
4	Google	15.7
6	eBay	12.7
8	Amazon	9.3
12	USA Networks: (Citysearch/Ticketmaster)	6.9

We might expect that search engines would draw the largest audiences. Following them, the most popular consumer sites are Amazon.com and eBay.com which routinely draw millions of visitors a month.

What's striking to me is that right after eBay and Amazon comes a group of sites operated by USA Networks. That company, which owns Ticketmaster, operates the twelfth most frequently visited network of sites on the Internet.

And according to comScore Media Metrix, in September 2002, Ticketmaster's site registered an increase in visits of 46.2% percent over the same time a year before.

Although Ticketmaster's main business is not involved with the arts, this phenomenal increase demonstrates the degree to which online ticketing has rapidly become integrated into the online shopping experience. We'll examine how arts patrons buy tickets online in the next chapter.

CHAPTER 4

Arts Patrons Online

How do arts patrons use the Internet?

Now that we've looked at overall consumer behavior online, let's focus more closely on a segment of the online audience—the <u>arts</u> audience. To do this, I'll rely largely on the results of a multi-year study of online arts patrons' behavior.

The responses we'll review derive from three separate surveys of arts patrons. The first was in late 1999, and the other two were in 2002, comprising a total of over 5,000 responses. Each of these studies examines subscribers to the CultureFinder.com online e-mail newsletter.

Once you've reviewed these statistics, you'll recognize that these patrons are very much like your best subscribers and donors. They are passionate about the arts, and participate frequently. These are the patrons that matter most.

We'll use their online behavior to serve as a benchmark for the behavior of other similar arts patrons nationwide. I'm not suggesting that all arts patrons resemble these people, nor am I suggesting that 100% of your patrons are similar to these people. Rather, I believe a portion of your audience today reflects this behavior, a percentage that will grow during the next few years.

For simplicity's sake, I'll refer to this audience as "CF Arts Patrons."

Demographics of CF Arts Patrons

Women tend to be the key influencers and decision-makers of arts event attendance and ticket purchase. Not surprisingly then, a majority of CF Arts Patrons are women, hovering at about 66%.

This audience is also highly educated. About two-thirds possess an education level that leads to or includes a college level degree. More importantly, 37% have graduate degrees of some kind. That compares with only 8.9% nationwide.[14]

This is a highly engaged arts audience. Those who had subscribed to the CultureFinder.com newsletter attended an average of 11.6 arts events during the last year, compared with an average of only 3.6 for the rest of the online audience. (Arts events were defined as classical music, opera, dance, theater, Broadway, art museums and art film.)

An even more striking result appears when we examine frequent theater attendees, people who claim to have attended over five theater events in the last year. Over 70% of these patrons claim they have attended more than 16 events, and 39.6% have gone more than 27 times. These people lead highly arts-immersed lives![15]

We found that the heavier-attending consumers (those who had attended seven or more events per year) comprised 17% of the online population, but represented 64% of attendance at U.S. cultural events over the past year.[16]

Thus, if you're aiming your marketing efforts at reaching potential new patrons, these frequent attendees are the people you want to reach.

So, as you read through the balance of this chapter and the next, I hope you'll be prompted to think about the degree to which your core audience mirrors the behavior of the CF Arts Patrons we'll examine.

Waking up, eating, logging on

Logging on to the Internet is now a regular part of CF Arts Patrons' daily lives. Virtually all of them log on at least once a day, with nearly half indicating they log on more regularly than that.

Figure 5[17]
Internet Sessions by Frequency

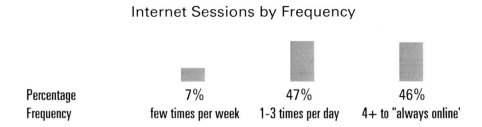

Percentage	7%	47%	46%
Frequency	few times per week	1-3 times per day	4+ to "always online'

The Internet is now seen as an integral communications medium, alongside other traditional media types. Arts patrons seem to be information seekers, reading newspaper articles and reviews most frequently.

Beyond this, traditional means of reaching them are just as frequently cited as the newer online methods.

Figure 6[18]
Sources of Information about Arts Events Near Home

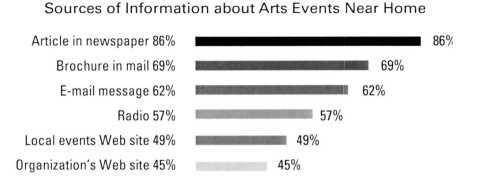

Article in newspaper 86% — 86%
Brochure in mail 69% — 69%
E-mail message 62% — 62%
Radio 57% — 57%
Local events Web site 49% — 49%
Organization's Web site 45% — 45%

And, once online, they buy

About 80% of CF Arts Patrons claim they buy something online each month. About 12% say they are very frequent buyers – making purchases a few times a week.

Figure 7[18]
Online Shopping Frequency

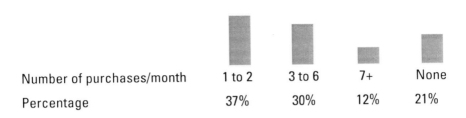

Number of purchases/month	1 to 2	3 to 6	7+	None
Percentage	37%	30%	12%	21%

Their buying habits reflect their arts-involved lifestyles.

Arts patrons tend to lead active, engaged lives and buy experiential and intellectual items. Books, CDs, travel and event tickets are among their most frequently purchased items.

Figure 8[20]
Types of Items Purchased During Past Six Months

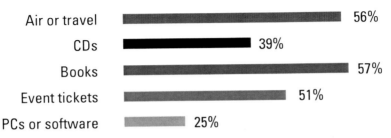

Air or travel	56%
CDs	39%
Books	57%
Event tickets	51%
PCs or software	25%

And, naturally, when they are online they buy arts tickets

Instructive and interesting patterns emerge when we analyze arts ticket buying preferences. We asked CF Art Patrons how they "most often" buy their arts tickets today, and then analyzed that data based on age.

Among arts patrons over 55 years old, 43% claim that they call the box office or a ticketing agency. About 19% say they go to the box office in person and 11% use the U.S. Post Office to send what is now commonly known as "snail-mail."

Interestingly, fewer than one in four of those over 55 claim they "most frequently" buy their arts tickets online.

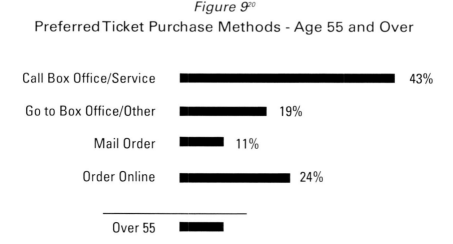

Figure 9[20]
Preferred Ticket Purchase Methods - Age 55 and Over

Call Box Office/Service	43%
Go to Box Office/Other	19%
Mail Order	11%
Order Online	24%
Over 55	

Younger arts patrons prefer the Web

The next generation of ticket buyers, those currently under 35, represent the "holy grail" for many arts marketers. This is the proverbial audience of the future.

When we look at their preferences, they show a dramatic increase in their desire to buy tickets online. Of this younger group, 43% claim they buy online—and every other traditional category is significantly diminished.

This younger audience is truly an online-centered group. My bet is that the percentage of people who prefer online ticket buying will increase during the next few years.

Figure 10[22]
Preferred Ticket Purchase Methods - Age 35 and Under

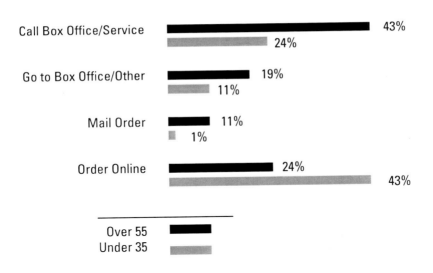

For audiences between 35 and 55 years old, 31% claimed they buy online most frequently. In fact, what's likely is that <u>all</u> age groups, the younger and the older audiences, will expand their online ticket buying as the shopping experience improves.

As arts executives and boards debate how to change the artistic product to attract a younger audience, perhaps the first place to start is by selling the product in a place where the younger audience prefers to buy it.

Moreover, Ticketmaster, which in 2001 sold 86 million tickets, has relatively quietly built an online sales operation that now accounts for 43% of its ticket inventory, an increase of 9% over 2001. No cover stories in *Time Magazine* have celebrated this radical shift in the way this company transacts its business, yet this is a staggering shift in the way consumers buy tickets, and it has happened in a very short period of time.

Let's correlate this buying data with actual recent sales data from the following arts organizations.

% of tickets sold online

New York Philharmonic	14.3%
Stamford Center for the Arts	10.0%
CAPA Chicago	29.5%
The New Victory Theater	8.0%

An interesting case history comes from the Victoria & Albert Museum in London. It periodically offers blockbuster exhibitions for which it sells tickets online. In 2001 it mounted an exhibition about Victorians for which 16% of the tickets sold in advance were purchased online. By comparison, in the spring and summer of 2002, just over a year later, a blockbuster exhibition about Versace sold a whopping 49% of its advanced tickets online.

CHAPTER 5

Introducing E-mail Marketing

Why e-mail matters so much

As we move into our discussion about e-mail marketing, I'd like to first dispel an all-too-common misunderstanding. Some discount the potential of e-mail marketing because they think people are getting too much e-mail already and that nobody wants any more if it.

Nothing is further from the truth.

Yes, consumers get a lot of e-mail and a good portion of it is unwanted commercial mail. That said, consumers have a very personal relationship with their "inbox," much more so than with their post office box. They know what's in there, and have developed well-worn decision-making rules that govern what they look at and respond to.

Fortunately, arts patrons view arts e-mail not as commercial mail, but rather like mail from their friends. They see arts organizations as an extension of their lifestyle, and the e-mail you send them is treated accordingly. Unlike direct mail that gets thrown out at home along with the Lands' End catalog, arts e-mail gets noticed and not deleted.

As such, e-mail arts marketing offers tremendous potential and has already begun to revolutionize the way some arts organizations do business.

With that in mind, let's explore this fascinating consumer relationship with e-mail.

What's the one thing that we know virtually all online consumers do every day?

Yes, they check their e-mail!

Indeed, e-mail dominates all other online activities, by orders of magnitude over other kinds of online activity.

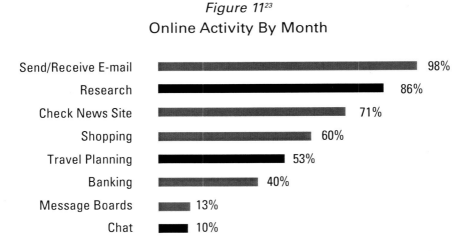

Figure 11[23]
Online Activity By Month

It's true that arts patrons get an increasing amount of e-mail.

In 2002, in the U.S. last year the U.S. Post Office delivered about 209 billion pieces of mail. Of that, 100 billion were first class mail and 9% were personal letters.[24] By comparison, about 840 billion pieces of e-mail were sent in 2002, a number which is predicted to rise to over one trillion by 2003.[25]

On average, CF Arts Patrons get 25 e-mail messages a day, and 12% of them get more than 50.

As we've seen before, arts patrons log on regularly, and when they do they check their e-mail. About 47% claim they check their mail one to three times a day, and 46% claim to check it more than three times daily. Only 7% aren't checking their inbox every day.

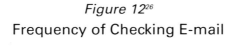

Figure 12[26]
Frequency of Checking E-mail

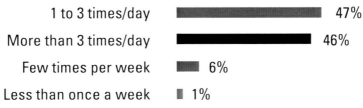

1 to 3 times/day	47%
More than 3 times/day	46%
Few times per week	6%
Less than once a week	1%

Not all e-mail is created equally

I divide the world of e-mail into two spheres. First there is personal mail: mail from co-workers, friends, spouses, relatives and others you know. I'm not going to discuss or analyze that type.

Rather, we'll focus entirely on commercial e-mail, which itself falls into two categories.

1. Commercial mass mailings: This is commonly known as "junk" or "Spam." This is mail sent by a company to whom you have not given explicit permission to communicate with you.
2. Opt-in: The other kind is known as "permission-based" or "opt-in" e-mail.

This is e-mail that you have personally taken the initiative to request by signing up on a Web site, or giving your name by phone, or on a sign-up sheet at a theater, etc. What's important here is that you personally chose to "opt-in."

Here's an example of the opt-in screen from The Whitney Museum of American Art.

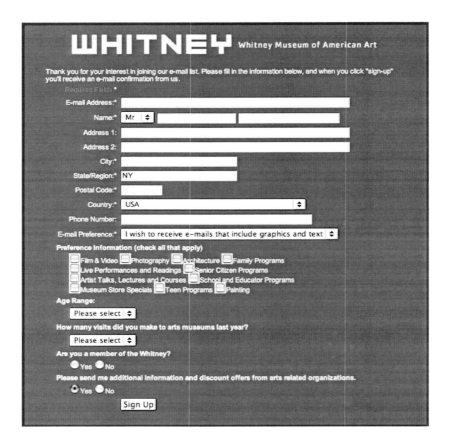

What's going on when a patron signs up for your newsletter is actually a very subtle transaction. It's a marketing transaction, although no money is changing hands. Patrons trade off something they value (their privacy and personal information) in return for your promise to first and foremost protect this information by not selling it to others, and then to send them valuable and relevant messages that may otherwise not be available to the general public.

As a result, when consumers receive opt-in e-mail, their reaction towards it differs dramatically from that of junk mail. Basically, patrons welcome opt-in e-mail and reject Spam.

Over two-thirds of CF Arts Patrons say that when they see a piece of opt-in e-mail in their inbox they are curious to read it. Only 2% claim that they delete opt-in e-mail before reading it.

Figure 13[27]
Reactions to Receipt of Opt-in E-mail

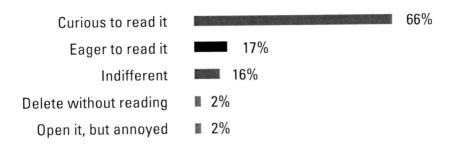

Curious to read it	66%
Eager to read it	17%
Indifferent	16%
Delete without reading	2%
Open it, but annoyed	2%

Now let's look at their reactions to junk mail. An overwhelming majority (84%) claim they delete junk mail without ever reading it.

Figure 14[28]
Reactions to Receipt of Spam

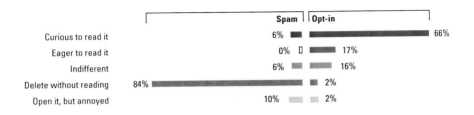

	Spam	Opt-in
Curious to read it	6%	66%
Eager to read it	0%	17%
Indifferent	6%	16%
Delete without reading	84%	2%
Open it, but annoyed	10%	2%

It seems that CF Arts Patrons are a highly discerning audience with a finely developed nose for what's in their inbox.

Spam has been, and will likely continue to be, a major annoyance. Industry estimates are that Spam accounted for 40% of all commercial mail in 2002, up from only 8% in 2001.[29] Although there are many aggressive anti-Spam efforts being made, none appears to be capable of making a significant dent in this problem.

However, as arts marketers, it's not something we need to focus on nearly as much as other kinds of commercial marketers. Your patrons value the e-mail you send them and don't see it as an annoyance.

Once subscribed, opt-in e-mail gets read!

What's most important about opt-in e-mail is that once patrons ask to receive it, a significant number read it. About 50% of CF Arts Patrons say they read opt-in e-mail "all the time" and just under half say they read it "occasionally/maybe." Importantly, only 5% claim they delete opt-in e-mail without ever reading it.

Overall, we would then assume that about half of your audience would be paying some kind of attention to e-mail messages you send. Compared to almost any other kind of marketing media, that's an incredible statistic.

We'll see evidence of this in our case histories in Chapter 7.

Before we leave the subject of arts patrons' relationship to e-mail, let's take an additional look by examining their psychographic attitudes towards e-mail, which provides a fascinating insight into what's going on.

There seems to be a more personal relationship to individual arts organizations than might be expected. This is demonstrated by the fact that 51% of CF Arts Patrons claim that they read opt-in arts e-mail *as carefully as they read mail from their friends.*

That's a pretty staggering result. How carefully do these same arts patrons read your direct mail? My sense is that though arts e-mail is commercial mail in some sense, a significant percentage of people perceive it in ways that are more personal than commercial.

Looking at how patrons read their e-mail on a continuum—where one side of the scale represents e-mail that always gets read (say e-mail from spouses, siblings, colleagues), and the other represents junk mail, which mostly doesn't get read—then arts e-mail seems to be in a unique and protected middle category.

What a wonderful opportunity for arts marketers to take advantage of!

Arts patrons are eager to get arts e-mail

CF Arts Patrons seem to be eager to receive e-mail from arts organizations. What's most encouraging is that their appetite is not limited to receiving e-mail from only those arts organizations to which they have a membership or subscription.

Rather, they seem to welcome communications from a wide range of institutions:

- Over half say that they would be interested in joining a mailing list for arts organizations that they have never attended before, but are interested in.
- About 60% said they would join a mailing list for an organiza-

tion in a city they don't live in, but visit regularly! So, for the first time ever, it's now cost-effective to market to someone in Philadelphia who comes to New York on a regular basis.

When you examine the following figures, I expect you'll recognize a host of expanded marketing opportunities.

Figure 15[30]

Likelihood of Joining E-mail Lists by Type of Organization

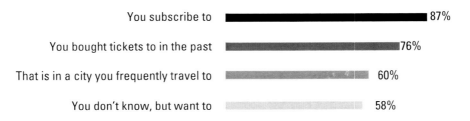

You subscribe to	87%
You bought tickets to in the past	76%
That is in a city you frequently travel to	60%
You don't know, but want to	58%

There's something else going on which explains these patrons' willingness to receive arts e-mail. CF Arts Patrons seem to understand well how financially strapped arts organizations are. They know how expensive it is to send regular mail, and innately understand that e-mail marketing can save organizations money.

This is demonstrated by the fact that 77% claim that because e-mail can save the arts organization money, they "feel good" by getting it. It's almost as if they believe they are making a donation by receiving arts e-mail!

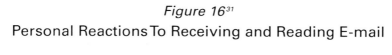

Figure 16[31]

Personal Reactions To Receiving and Reading E-mail

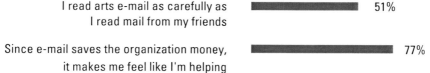

I read arts e-mail as carefully as
I read mail from my friends   51%

Since e-mail saves the organization money,   77%
it makes me feel like I'm helping

Arts patrons prefer e-mail

For a surprisingly large percentage of CF Arts Patrons e-mail is the preferred method of communication.

This chart compares CF Arts Patrons' interest in getting marketing messages by e-mail versus direct mail, as well as their reactions to receiving e-mail versus telemarketing. The dramatic preference for e-mail suggests that by e-mailing these patrons first, in advance of a telemarketing campaign, you will reduce your telemarketing costs and improve your response rates.

Figure 17[32]

E-mail Preference vs. Other Marketing Methods

I would prefer to get e-mail notices
rather than direct mail   23%   37%   60%

I would prefer to get e-mail notices
rather than telemarketing calls   8%   82%   90%

somewhat agree   strongly agree

Arts e-mail has multiple lives

Arts e-mail is more valuable than other kinds of marketing because the "shelf life" of e-mail is longer and the uses of e-mail are many. Compared to newspapers that get thrown away in a day or two, radio messages that last a few seconds or direct mail which likely ends up in the garbage, an e-mail message has many lives.

Here are some ways that patrons extend the life of an e-mail message:

- Forward to a friend: Over 60% of CF Arts Patrons report that they have forwarded e-mail to their friends in the last month. This makes sense, since the arts are typically a communal experience. Forwarding an e-mail to a friend in a click or two, with an invitation to go to a event or exhibition can motivate a later transaction.

- Read now, act later: About half claim they use the e-mail for information purposes when they open it, only to purchase later.

- E-mail transforms into direct mail: Over 45% claim they print out an e-mail and save it for later. In this case your patron has essentially converted your e-mail into direct mail, only you've shifted the printing and postage cost onto her! That e-mail then serves the same purpose as a direct mail flyer or postcard. It goes into her briefcase or purse, or on her desk or refrigerator until she's ready to take action.

Arts patrons welcome contact

Many arts marketers worry about mailing too much, for fear that they will drive their audience away. This is because they confuse opt-in mail with their personal distaste for Spam.

Remember, arts patrons don't view this e-mail as junk mail, rather they welcome hearing from you. More than one third expect that when they sign up for a mailing list, they will hear from the organization on a weekly basis. Virtually all expect something at least monthly.

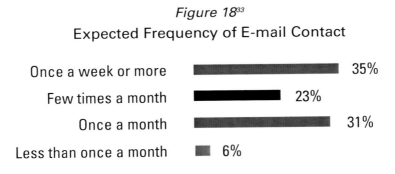

Figure 18[33]
Expected Frequency of E-mail Contact

Once a week or more — 35%
Few times a month — 23%
Once a month — 31%
Less than once a month — 6%

Last summer, The Public Theater in New York began collecting e-mail addresses from people waiting on line in Central Park for tickets to its annual "Free Shakespeare in the Park" series. Regular mailings weren't planned until the fall, but interestingly, they heard (by e-mail) from a few people who wrote in a week or two later saying "hey, I signed up for your newsletter – now where is it?"

A quick scan of about 50 arts organizations that actively utilize PatronMail shows that they e-mail their audiences about 2.5 times per month. I believe that these arts marketers could be mailing even more frequently, without any risk of alienating their patrons.

CHAPTER 6

By the Numbers

How the math works in your favor

Before we can get into a discussion about the true return on invest-ment (ROI) benefit of e-mail marketing, we need to understand the metrics of e-mail response rate tracking. These basic measures should help our understanding of how this medium works, and will inform our review of several case histories. A more detailed explanation of these terms can be found in the Glossary.

Open Rate: The open rate refers to the percentage of patrons who receive an e-mail and view it. Open rates are a measure of the interest level your audience has in your mailings. The range of open rates for all PatronMail clients during the last six months ranged between 35% and 60%.

Click-through Rate: This is the number of clicks on a specific link within an e-mail.

With this basic understanding, let's look at a hypothetical direct mail campaign vs. a similar campaign executed by e-mail. This hypo-thetical yet entirely reasonable example will show the dramatic improvement in ROI that can be achieved with e-mail marketing.

Assume you are the marketing director for an arts organization, and you've got an event for which you would like to sell tickets at $45 each. Let us further assume that each household will buy a pair of tickets, and that you've got a mailing list of 10,000 names and addresses—both home addresses, and opt-in e-mail addresses.

Direct Mail Approach

You take a two-week period to write copy, submit it to a designer, review different approaches and approve a version that gets sent to the printer. You get back the printed material and mail it out a week later.

When you add up design costs, printing, postage, mail-shop (excluding the cost of staff time) your total comes to about $1.20 per piece including postage. You send 10,000 pieces, at a total cost of $12,000.

After another two weeks, you get a respectable response rate of 1.5% yielding a sale of 300 tickets, generating revenue of $13,500. You are pleased as this effort has not only helped fill empty seats, but has also netted the organization $1,500. Your ROI here is 12.5%.

E-mail Approach

You start by spending an hour preparing the e-mail message, by writing copy, uploading images and formatting. Your cost to send, using prevailing PatronMail pricing, is about $360. You send it out later that day.

Within three hours you start getting results, and within 48 hours you get a click-through rate of 10% to the link that says "click here to buy tickets online." Then, within 72 hours you detect that 25% of those who clicked ultimately bought tickets.

That number includes all those that clicked and purchased immediately, as well as those who forwarded the e-mail to a friend and purchased later, called the box office, or printed out the e-mail and took it to the box office. We're looking here at an overall 2.5% response rate, a result that we have seen with many clients.

This generates a sale of 250 tickets, and $22,000 of income. You have netted $21,640, an ROI of over 6,000%.

If there's only one page of this book that makes the point about the ROI of e-mail marketing, this is it.

	Direct Mail	E-mail
Cost to Send	$12,000	$360
Open Rate	unknown	45%
Response Rate	1.5%	10% click-through; 25% of those buy
Sales/Tickets	300 tickets	500 tickets
Revenue Generated	$13,500	$22,500
Time Elapsed	3 weeks	48 hours

CHAPTER 7

Results from the Real World

What does success look like?

Perhaps the best way to understand this medium is by looking at some case studies. I've selected a few PatronMail client campaigns to give you a flavor for actual open and click-through rates. Then, two colleagues will present their own case histories, demonstrating the kinds of positive ROI results alluded to earlier.

Case Study: The Whitney Museum of American Art – Biennial Exhibition Announcement

In March 2002, the Whitney Museum sent an e-newsletter to 10,000 members and non-members. The purpose was to announce the opening of their Biennial exhibition, drive traffic to the resources on its Web site and motivate visits to the exhibition.

The first article included a link to the exhibition, and the second allowed patrons to download a specially commissioned digital work of art to a Palm Pilot. The open rate was 47.5%, and the overall click-through rate was 13.3%. Furthermore, 5.5% of the recipients clicked the link to download the artwork.

The Whitney's biennial announcement, March 2002:

WHITNEY Whitney Museum of American Art

Exhibition News March 7, 2002

The 2002 Biennial opens today!

Download a tap-dancing work of art

Walk under a 50-foot stainless steel tree

Catch a screening of Dennis Hopper's latest video

Dance to a live performance

11 WEEKS,
113 ARTISTS,
HUNDREDS OF EVENTS

Inside this email you'll find a sampling of the extraordinary range of works now on view at this year's Whitney Biennial.

The 2002 Biennial opens today!

The Whitney Biennial brings you the latest in American art, including the largest presentation of performance, sound art, film, video, and architecture ever presented in a Biennial, as well as painting, drawing, sculpture, and large-scale installations.

Ari Marcopoulos, "Stockholm," 1999

Learn more about the 2002 Biennial Exhibition

Download a tap-dancing work of art

Internet art, which made its first Biennial appearance in the 2000 show, this year includes an artwork that can be "beamed" to visitors' handheld PDA devices from a beaming station in the Museum Lobby.

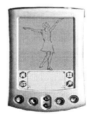

James Buckhouse, in collaboration with Holly Brubach, "Tap," 2002

Learn more or download "Tap"

Walk under a 50-foot stainless steel tree

For the first time, the Biennial moves outdoors to Central Park, organized by the Public Art Fund, with five major artists' projects including a 50-foot-tall metal "tree." Tours are given in April and May through a collaboration with the Central Park Conservancy. For dates and times, call the Dairy Visitor Center at (212) 794-6564.

Learn more about the Whitney Biennial in Central Park

Catch a screening of Dennis Hopper's latest video

Film and video screenings across a range of different themes and genres are presented with the 2002 Biennial, including nontraditional documentary, animation, and narrative and abstract cinema.

View full screening schedule

Dance to a live performance

The Biennial's sound and performance program is a constellation of unique and ongoing events. Pick up a complete performance schedule in the Museum Lobby. To see the schedule for upcoming Fridays, including a musical and theatrical spectacle by Gogol Bordello, the ensemble whose self-described style is "Ukrainian Gypsy punk cabaret," click on the link below.

Case Study: Mann Center for the Arts
—Renewal Early Bird Notice

In an effort to motivate early ticket sales for its upcoming season, the Mann Center sent out an e-mail offering a 10% discount off the regular ticket price if patrons purchased a month before the full season schedule was announced, and tickets were made available to the public.

Note that this was an exclusive offer to the e-mail list, offering real value to subscribers beyond what they could get as a member of the general public.

The open rate was 59.5%. Of those that opened the e-mail, the click through rate was 29.8%. The overall click-through rate was 17%.

Case Study: The New Victory Theater
—Renewal Campaign

This case history is provided by Janice Chaikelson, Director of Marketing for The New Victory Theater.

The New Victory Theater, www.newvictory.org, a presenting house for kids and family programming in New York City, used both online and direct mail methods for its renewal Membership campaign this year, but eliminated phone-based renewals. Thus, the only methods of renewal available for the first two months of the campaign were by Web or by mailing or faxing an order form from the direct mail piece.

The arrival of the direct mail piece was preceded by an e-mail sent directly from the theater to prospective renewals. The e-mail stated that a brochure would follow shortly by mail, but that all the information could be accessed immediately on the Web site and that orders could be placed there right away. The e-mail included a link to the site.

A postcard with the same information was also sent directly to prospective renewals whose e-mail addresses were not on record. (The postcard made it known that computer terminals would be set up in the theater lobby in order to give those with no Internet access the same chance to order early as those who had Internet access at home or at work.) In response, about 660 orders were placed in the two weeks prior to the receipt of the brochure, representing a 15% renewal rate.

Once the direct mail hit, the combination of the two mediums created an interaction that drove the balance of the sales. We cannot, however, determine precisely which medium ultimately motivated the sale, or whether it was the combination of the two.

THE NEW VICTORY™ THEATER

ORDER YOUR 2002-03 SEASON MEMBER TICKETS EARLY - ONLINE!
Exclusively for 2001-02 Members

9 Fabulous Shows For 2002-03!

An updated WWW.NEWVICTORY.ORG launches on Monday, July 8 at 8am complete with all the season information you'll need for ordering and a new, easy to use shoppng cart ordering process.

Click the link below for immediate access to the New Victory website -- www.newvictory.org -- where you'll get all the information on the 9 fabulous shows in the 2002-03 season. Plus, you'll have access to video clips, expanded articles about every show, and family activities. With the new, shopping cart format order form, ordering online is even easier than before! The website also offers the following conveniences:
- 24 hours a day access
- emailed order confirmations
- daily updates of ticket availabilty (sold out performances and/or theater sections are removed from the order form so that you cannot select a sold out option)
- the option to pay by check
- the ability to order all your tickets at once: Member tickets, additional full price tickets, birthday party tickets and VicTeens tickets

You should be receiving your brochure in a couple of weeks. Take this advance opportunity and order online STARTING MONDAY!
I'm Ready To Order Online! Take Me To The New Victory Website!

To be removed from future mailings, reply with REMOVE in the subject line or click here.

If you would like to change your e-mail preferences or update your e-mail address, click here.

What we do know is that the investment in online technology was about $15,000, versus the overall revenue that came in from orders placed over the Web of nearly $700,000.

The cost per piece for the brochure was $.78 per address. The e-mail cost was about $.03 per address, and the postcard to prospective renewals for whom e-mail addresses were not known was about $.23.

Finally, and perhaps most unexpectedly, <u>72% of members this season signed up via the Web,</u> thus proving that Web/e-mail can be an inexpensive part of an overall marketing mix, providing an immediate and tangible call to action.

Case Study: Goodspeed Musicals —Renewal Campaign

Dan McMahon, Director of Marketing & Public Relations for Goodspeed Musicals provides this report.

Every fall, Goodspeed Musicals sets out to renew our members and subscribers, as our season ends in December and begins the following spring.

In past years, membership was renewed first, using direct mail. Once a member renewed they were then sent subscription renewal information. The reason for the two-step process was because traditional benefits, such as seat location, are tied to the membership level. Subscription, therefore, is a benefit of membership.

In 2002 a new approach was taken in an effort to streamline the process and make it easier for both the member/subscriber and the Goodspeed staff. A key ingredient of the new process was to test the Internet for renewal. The benefits of doing so are obvious: lower printing and mailing cost in addition to faster response. At risk was potentially losing members/subscribers and the fact that our audience skews older and we were not sure of their Internet habits.

First, we created our list to include only member/subscribers at the lowest donor levels and those whom we had e-mail addresses for. Next, we created a stand-alone, secure Web site for renewal. The site was interactive and personalized. Patron information as well as subscription details were included on the site.

Patrons logged in with their password, reviewed their information, chose their new donor level (pop up boxes encouraged them to increase their gift from the previous year), renewed their subscription (with space for requesting seat changes, etc.), reviewed their renewal information and payment method. Payment by credit card was encouraged. Since some prefer to donate by check, there was also a system for that. Once renewed, an automatic e-mail was sent to confirm receipt of their renewal order. The site was simple, clear and user-friendly.

The marketing process began with an e-mail alerting the patron to watch their e-mail box for their personalized renewal packet. The following week, a customized e-mail was sent that contained their unique password and a link to the renewal site.

We worked with Patron Technology to allow us to merge name information and password information linked to e-mail addresses. This allowed for a personalized e-mail.

Without the personalized e-mail, we would not have been able to renew online. We had to send each individual a unique password so they would be the only person to access their information on the renewal site. The only other way to achieve this would have been to mail the password, but that would have defeated the purpose. We theorized that people would be curious enough to click directly to the site and that we were providing customer service by making the process very easy.

We viewed daily reports through our PatronMail account to track usage. It was very exciting to see how many had opened the e-mail and how many had clicked through to the site. Such a huge benefit over direct mail! Instead of just knowing a response rate based on orders, we know how many patrons actually opened our e-mail! At the box office we were able to track renewal orders daily.

Once the click-through rate fell off, after about 10 days, we sent a reminder e-mail that was a bit more aggressive in pushing the renewal deadline. Again we watched the results daily. When click-through fell off again, we sent a final reminder.

After the final reminder, our telemarketing department called those who had not responded. We also surveyed each patron about their awareness of the online renewal program, why they did not use it, and their communication preferences for the future.

Our analysis of the results rates this test as an unqualified success. 47% of our test group of member/subscribers renewed online. Using standard renewal methods our final renewal rate will exceed 85%. However, we were able to renew almost half of the test group with relatively little effort and very little cost.

In addition, the positive comments greatly outweighed the negative comments. Most patrons applauded our using the Internet for renewal and for combining our renewal of membership and subscription at the same time. One final benefit was to wrap up the renewal process for the test group in eight weeks as opposed to 16 weeks for our traditional campaign.

Analysis of each e-mail that was sent revealed some interesting results. We had no idea what the pattern would be. What we found is that the open rate for each e-mail was similar (#1: 56%, #2: 56%, #3: 52%). The click-through rate was similar for the first two e-mails (#1:52% of those who opened the e-mail, #2: 50%).

However, the click-through rate fell for the third e-mail: 22%. Not knowing what to expect, we were happy that half of our patrons opened the e-mail and went to the renewal site. We were disappointed, however, that more did not open the e-mail. Our telephone survey has not been processed, but reading through them we find that the biggest problem was that they did not know what the e-mail was about (despite that fact that the subject was "Goodspeed Renewal") so they didn't open or deleted it.

Regarding click-through rates, the largest group of those who had opened the e-mail, but did not continue, said that they preferred to renew by mail or telephone.

For those who clicked through and actually went to the site, it seems from the telephone survey that some did not understand how to use their password. Others were afraid to use their credit card online.

The telephone survey allows us incredible information for planning next year's campaign. From the test group, we can now segment our patrons by communication preference (i.e. renew online, by mail, by phone) which will surely enhance our efforts, raise our renewal rate and reduce expenses.

It is interesting to note that most of the patrons in the survey who did not open the e-mail said they would like to get the information electronically next year, now that they understood what it was all about. We believe that our older audience is not as Internet savvy as younger patrons, but they are interested in using the Internet. We also believe that in one year's time, their comfort with the Internet, and with purchasing on the Internet, will greatly increase.

For next year's campaign we already know that we need to better prepare our patrons for the idea of renewing online, simplify passwords, and reassure them even more about using credit cards on the Internet.

This was a great learning experience for both our patrons and us. It really provides great information for moving more and more toward using the Internet to communicate with our patrons, cutting mailing costs, and improving segmentation.

CHAPTER 8

Gene's Smart Tips
For E-mail Marketing

What you need to know to get started properly

If you're convinced that e-mail marketing is the way to go, what should you do next? I've prepared a list of tips outlining the most basic things you need to do properly to achieve the kinds of results we've just seen.

All of these tips presuppose that you utilize professional software to do e-mail marketing. Microsoft Outlook and other desktop software were designed mainly to enable individuals to write to one person or a small group of people at a time, and not created to serve as a powerful marketing tool.

Ultimately, to do this kind of e-mail marketing effectively will require that you utilize the proper tool for the job. Needless to say, our PatronMail software has been designed to address all of the issues that I'll cover in this section. PatronMail is far from the only software product on the market, however, it uniquely addresses the particular needs of the arts market. So, as you read through these tips, please understand that I assume the use of professional e-mail marketing software.

Gene's Smart Tip # 1: Make the development of your "opt-in" e-mail list a major marketing objective.

As in direct mail marketing, success starts first and foremost with having a great list. And, in this case, you need a great opt-in list. You cannot execute effective e-mail marketing without it. It's that simple.

Unfortunately, there are no short cuts to building an opt-in list. You can't buy an "arts multi-ticket buyer" e-mail list sorted by zip code. Privacy concerns (which we will discuss in Chapter 10) have prevented this kind of marketplace from developing.

And, if you know of an e-mail list for sale, it's probably not worth buying. Some unscrupulous vendors sell lists of names that were compiled by violating privacy policies. Others claim to have 100% opt-in lists. However, in our experience those lists are so broad as to be hardly useful as a cost-effective way of identifying the kinds of arts patrons you are seeking.

The good news, as we've demonstrated earlier, is that your patrons are eager to sign-up for e-mail communications from you. And, it is that very act of "opting in" that influences consumer expectations and reactions to your e-mail.

To build your list, you must make an institutional commitment to doing this properly. You need to have the cooperation of everyone in the organization who communicates directly with your patrons, and you need to develop and execute an overall plan for collecting names.

The single largest reason I see for organizations failing to collect significant numbers of e-mail names is merely a lack of aggressiveness.

I encourage you to collect e-mail names at every opportunity and with every contact with your patrons for the next few years. Each of the following represents an opportunity to ask for an e-mail sign-up:

- At your venue in the lobby and in public areas
- Through inserts in programs
- In the parking lot
- At the box office: When taking a ticket order, your box-office staff can easily request this information. (Many box offices can't handle this work two hours before an event. But you can at least mandate that this information be collected at other times.)
- Within renewal or new subscriptions campaigns

Case Study: CAPA
—E-mail List Building Effort

This case study is provided by Jim Hirsch, Vice President and Executive Director of the Chicago Association for the Performing Arts.

The Chicago Association for the Performing Arts (CAPA) is the not-for-profit presenting organization that manages the 3,600-seat Chicago Theatre at 175 N. State Street in downtown Chicago. CAPA also owns three large theaters in downtown Columbus, Ohio and manages three others for the State of Ohio as the Columbus Association for the Performing Arts. It also manages and programs the Shubert Theatre in New Haven, Connecticut as the Connecticut Association for the Performing Arts. Over ten million patrons attend events annually at CAPA-managed theaters.

We began building our database of e-mail addresses in late 2000 using a few simple tactics. Initially, most of the addresses were collected through lobby intercepts. Ushers would invite audience members to fill out e-mail/address cards. We employed incentives with audience members to sign-up by conducting contests for free dinners, tickets or airline tickets at each show. Signage was created to support the contests.

This method typically garnered collection of e-mail addresses from 5-10% of the total attendance at each show. For a sold-out event

(3,553 people), we would collect 150-350 e-mail addresses.

In addition, the CAPA Web site (www.capa.com) was altered to allow browsers to sign up for the program online, and print and radio advertising for shows began including information about the eCAPA program. Using the tactics noted above CAPA was able to build the database to 4,000 names by the spring of 2001.

During late 2001 and into early 2002, CAPA began to experiment with other collection tactics as a way of building the size of the database, including:

- During shows promoted by CAPA, a pre-show announcement explained the eCAPA program to the audience and encouraged them to sign up during intermission and after the show.
- Realizing the difficulty of approaching audience members individually, explaining the program and urging them to sign up, especially during the sold-out events when the lobby became loud and crowded, CAPA printed up simple flyers explaining eCAPA and giving a space to write the e-mail address. The flyer explained that the completed form could be placed in a lobby box or handed to an usher. The flyer also included the Web address for online sign-up.
- Enter-to-win contests on Metromix (the Tribune Company's entertainment Web site), Viva Radio (an Hispanic music station) and in *Exito!* (The Tribune's Spanish language newspaper). These tactics did not generate significant sign-ups.
- An enter-to-win contest during a two-night run of *Prince* called "Winners in the House" that generated 1,000 e-mail addresses.
- A ticket give-away promotion with all 22 Borders Books stores in the Chicago area for which people had to fill out an entry form to enter. This contest garnered 247 e-mail addresses from over 1,000 entries.

- CAPA installed a computer in the lobby for sign-ups at the box office during regular business hours and during events. By early spring of 2003, CAPA had collected 24,000 e-mail addresses and had begun using this list to sell tickets. Two specific results were notable:

  1. In May of 2002, CAPA presented Ellen DeGeneres. The eCAPA announcement sold 818 tickets for over $40,000 on one e-mail before any paid advertising or other announcements had been used.

  2. In July of 2002, CAPA hosted the Chicago Premiere of Dreamworks' "Road to Perdition." The studio gave CAPA 50 tickets to give away. We received over 1,500 requests in less than 24 hours.

Gene's Smart Tip # 2: Always collect segmentation and demographic information along with the e-mail address.

The most important rule of direct marketing is that the closer you come to matching a potential consumer's needs with an offer that meets those needs, the more successful you'll be in getting them to respond.

The crucial difference is that in mass marketing we essentially treat everyone the same and hope that the consumers we care about notice our message.

In direct marketing, we attempt to learn as much as we can about a consumer on a one-to-one basis, before we market to them.

For instance, I recently read an article about a company that plans to develop electronic billboards whose messages, as you drive by, are based on what you're listening to on your car radio. So, if you are listening to classical music, the symphony's ad appears on the billboard.

The premise here is the same. The more data you have about your patrons' interests, the more you can segment (or categorize) your mailings to get the best response rates. As an example, many arts institutions produce events geared for children, in an effort to develop the audiences for the future. When you send notices of children's events to patrons you already know are parents, they are more likely to respond than would a more generic list.

With proper e-mail marketing software, you can do this kind of marketing in a much easier way than in direct mail. <u>All you have to do is ask your customers to tell you up-front what interests them, and you can then market directly to them!</u>

The moment at which a patron is signing-up for your mailing list is when you have the most leverage to extract information from them. Essentially, the information they give you is the "price tag" for the promise of the benefits your e-mail communication promises. However, you must collect this information as they sign up for the first time, or it's nearly impossible to get it later.

On CultureFinder.com, beyond basic personal information, we ask six preference and demographic questions on the sign-up screen. On average, 89% of the patrons fill out some or all of these questions, even though it is not mandatory that they do so.

However, our experience shows that if you attempt to ask people these kinds of marketing questions after-the-fact, your response rates will be slim. Many organizations have existing lists for which they have no demographic data, and send an e-mail to solicit it. We've seen response rates range from 10% to 30%. Basically, at the moment of sign-up, you have one chance to get patrons to give you this information, so don't miss it.

The first place to accumulate sign-ups is on your Web site, by placing a prominent button (circled in the following example) on the main screen of your site, and on all interior pages.

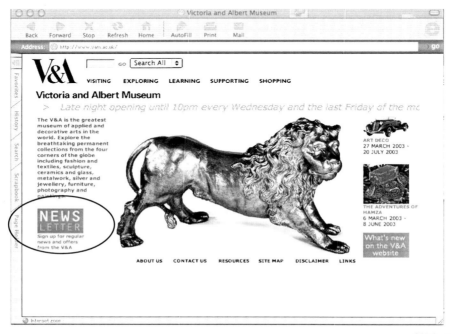

©V & A

An even more effective approach is to arrange for a pop-up screen to appear the first time a patron visits your site. When we adopted this approach on the CultureFinder.com site, we instantly increased our daily sign-ups fivefold.

We find that patrons will willingly answer about four to five questions during the sign-up process. Here is an example of a sign-up screen.

CALIFORNIA MUSICAL THEATRE

Thank you for your interest in joining our e-mail list. Please fill in the information below, and when you click "sign-up" you'll receive an e-mail confirmation from us.

Required Fields *

E-mail Address:* [ ]

Name:* [Mr ⬍] [ ] [ ]

Address 1: [ ]

Address 2: [ ]

City:* [ ]

State/Region:* [CA]

Postal Code:* [ ]

Country:* [USA ⬍]

Phone Number: [ ]

E-mail Preference:* [I wish to receive e-mails that include graphics and text ⬍]

Your email address is from:

○ Home ○ School ○ Work

Your phone number is from:

○ Home ○ Work

Information Preference (check all that apply)

☐ Music Circus schedule and news ☐ Broadway Series schedule and news
☐ Auditions ☐ Education programs ☐ Membership and fund-raising
☐ Volunteering

Age Range

○ Under 12 ○ 13 - 17 ○ 18 - 24 ○ 25 - 34 ○ 35 - 49 ○ 50 - 64 ○ 65 and over

Have you attended the Music Circus before?

○ Yes ○ No

Have you attended the Broadway Series before?

○ Yes ○ No

Are there children living in your home?

○ Yes ○ No

Are you within driving distance of Sacramento?

○ Yes ○ No

I would like to receive information and discount offers from other arts organizations that California Musical Theatre works with.

○ Yes ⦿ No

[Sign Up]

Gene's Smart Tip # 3: Send targeted e-mail messages.

Now that you've collected all this rich demographic and preference information, your e-mails should be as targeted as possible.

Picking up from our example before, let's say that 15% of your e-mail subscribers have children under the age of 12 living with them. An e-mail with a special to them for your next children's event might include a subject line such as "Parents: Whitney Kids Weekend – Feb. 28."

Alternatively, if you produce events in a wide variety of genres and know which people are interested in musicals, as opposed to baroque music or modern dance, then you can send them messages specifically tailored to their interests.

Sending targeted messages has a secondary benefit. It communicates a subtle message to your patrons that you know and respect their interests. In other words, you're building trust with them, demonstrating that your organization's e-mail isn't Spam! The more you send targeted messages, the more you will train your audience to believe that your e-mail messages are worth looking at and opening.

Given that sending e-mail is so inexpensive, you can easily send four different versions of the same mailing to four subsets of your mailing list and vary only the headline or an article within each, based on their particular interests.

Gene's Smart Tip #4: Care for your list.

Aside from creating it in the first place, maintaining and updating your e-mail list is the next most critical element of e-mail marketing. List maintenance includes bounced mail, opt-outs, and address updates.

Ideally, every e-mail message should offer the recipient a <u>one-click</u> way of removing herself from your list, or updating her profile or e-mail address. An instruction at the bottom of an e-mail that says "to opt out of this list send a blank e-mail to the following address with the word 'remove' in the subject line" was acceptable a few years ago, but frankly this asks too much of today's e-mail recipients. Even if they don't opt out, seeing a well placed opt-out link on the bottom of your e-mail will instill a sense of trust.

Bounced e-mail is e-mail that doesn't reach its intended recipient. There are many reasons for bounced e-mail. If you change your e-mail address (by canceling your AOL account for instance) your mail will "bounce back" since it cannot be delivered. Approximately 32% of all e-mail addresses change each year, resulting in an average bounce rate of 2.4% per month,[34] a rate that you should expect if you mail regularly.

There are dozens of other reasons why e-mail may bounce, which makes managing bounces as much an art as a science. An automatic "out-of-office" message will cause e-mail to bounce, even though the address is current. If Internet network traffic prevents an e-mail from being delivered immediately, the e-mail may bounce, but you don't want to remove that address from your list.

On average, 53% of all bounces are due to full inboxes or server outages, while 47% result from bad or non-existent addresses.[35] Again, professional software that is continually responsive to the ever-changing types of bounced e-mail is the only way to properly deal with this issue.

Opt-outs are recipients who have requested to be removed from your list. The percentage of patrons that opt out indicates the degree to which your e-mails are appreciated and/or annoying to your recipients.

Generally speaking, opt-outs are not much of a problem for arts organizations. Once you get patrons to join your list, they tend to stay. Across all of PatronMail clients, the opt-out rate for the first six months of 2002 was less than 1% percent.

Gene's Smart Tip #5: Send E-mail formatted in HTML.

E-mail can be sent in a variety of formats that affect what the recipient sees in their inbox. The two most popular formats are HTML, which displays graphics, pictures and copy, and "text-only."

From a marketing point-of-view, the most effective of these is HTML, with industry research showing that HTML messages have response rates up to twice that of text-only messages. The average click-through rates for text-only e-mails is 5.6%, while HTML returns click-through rates of 11.2%.[36]

However, not all e-mail software can render HTML e-mail properly. Some early versions of Lotus Notes and other older software can only display text e-mail messages. Early versions of AOL (before AOL version 6.0) interpret only certain aspects of HTML, excluding graphics and pictures.

Naturally, the arts are often about images and HTML provides a much richer opportunity to inform your audience about what you're doing than does text. Sending out text-only e-mail sends an unprofessional message. It's the cyber-equivalent of creating your season brochure on your desktop computer and copying it at Kinko's before mailing it out. Our research shows that about 80% of CF Arts Patrons prefer the HTML format. In the fourth quarter of 2002, only 9% of all commercial e-mail was in text format.[37]

Unfortunately, sending HTML e-mail is much easier said than done. Even if you have someone on your staff that knows HTML, this will not ensure that every recipient will be able to see your e-mail as you expect them to.

If you send an HTML e-mail message to a text-only e-mail client, the recipient will see gibberish. The only way to solve this is to use software especially developed to detect which kind of e-mail client is receiving the e-mail and which provides the appropriately formatted message.

Unfortunately, many marketers don't fully understand this subtlety, and believe that just because it looks fine on their PC it is working for all recipients. Ultimately, this is rather sophisticated stuff and that's why using professional software is essential.

Gene's Smart Tip #6: Measure, measure and measure!

The most interesting part of e-mail marketing comes when you begin to measure your response rates. Over time you will be able to learn from your campaigns what works with your audience – on what days of the week your patrons respond best, what kinds of discounts and offers they react most to, as well as what information is of no interest to them.

The following is a report from a recent campaign showing response rates to an e-mail newsletter with several links within it. Note the varying interest levels to each link.

◎ Campaign Detail

Campaign Name: **Lab Theatre E-News**
Date Sent: **2/11/2003**
Last Statistics Update: Monday March 24, 2003 8:00:02 AM
Glossary of terms

	Number	E-mail sent	E-mail opened
Campaign Results			
E-mail Messages Sent	3,001		
E-mail Messages Opened	1,252	42.6%	
Unique Patron Clicks	71	2.4%	5.7%
Click-thru Analysis			
Link(s)			
For complete schedule click... View Link	71	2.4%	5.7%
To order tickets click here View Link	26	0.9%	2.1%
To visit our web site click... View Link	11	0.4%	0.9%
Total Click-Thrus	**108**		
List Activity			
Bounced E-Mails View Details	57	1.9%	
Opt-outs View Details	6	0.2%	0.5%
Referrals / Conversions	4 / 2	0.1% (50.0%)	0.3%

As you can see, the software provides an updated report of all the aspects of your campaigns that have been discussed earlier in this book. Once you begin to see these results over time, you'll develop expertise on how to ensure the very best results for each mailing you send out.

CHAPTER 9

Effective E-Mail Marketing Strategy

Mapping out an e-mail marketing plan

Effective e-mail marketing requires an overall strategy. I recommend developing an annual plan, much as any magazine or newspaper would lay out its editorial plan for upcoming issues.

This will involve the selection and timing of a combination of the various types of e-mail messages. I'd like to focus on the two main types that you'll use:

- Information-oriented "e-newsletters"
- Action-oriented "e-postcards"

Information-Oriented E-Newsletter

Regular communication from an institution to its members is at the heart of a long-term loyalty building strategy. Most organizations don't have the funds to create a printed newsletter each month, but e-mail can serve this purpose.

Therefore, an e-mail newsletter is the basic building block for any e-mail marketing strategy. What's most important here is that these mailings are regularly scheduled and consistent in content, look and value.

Whether you send them every week, every month, or every two months, these mailings provide a "base level" of communication to your subscribers that makes up the heart of your online relationship.

e-Newsletter   **November 2002**

In This Issue:

What does the word STOMP make you think of?

Come enjoy the superb musicianship of Fourplay!

An Annual Holiday Tradition - Charles Dickens' A Christmas Carol

Shubert Corporate Club
Event Reminder
Contact Bridget for tickets
203-624-1825 or bcarmichael@capa.com

Shubert Theater Season Schedule

What does the word STOMP make you think of?

November 8-10, 2002
Limited Seating!!

Music, Dance, Theatre, Choreography or Performance Art? All of the above! Or is it none of the above. Well, both are sort of right... In a way. Confused? Follow the link below to read on...

http://www.shubert.com/shows/stomp/

Come enjoy the superb musicianship of Fourplay!

Thursday, November 14 at 8:00pm
Part of the United Technologies Holiday Series

Bob James - Keyboards
Harvey Mason - Drums
Nathan East - Bass
Larry Carlton - Guitar

Comprised of four of the worlds most revered and accomplished individual recording and performing artist's, the number of industry awards, honors and critical appellations received by both the individuals and the group as a whole, confirms their superlative reputation. Combining elements of R & B, pop, rock, blues, classical and jazz, Fourplay has managed to garner a legion of fans that literally spans all ethnic, musical and geographical boundaries.

Click here for more show information

An Annual Holiday Tradition - Charles Dickens' A Christmas Carol

November 29 - December 1, 2002
Part of the United Technologies Holiday Series

The Shubert Theater will present a musical adaptation of Charles Dickens' A Christmas Carol during the Thanksgiving weekend. This fully-staged musical follows the story of the miserly Ebeneezer Scrooge and the spirits of Christmas Past, Present and Future.

Click here for more event information

To order your tickets to these events or more, please contact Bridget Carmichael at 203-624-1825 ext. 315 or bcarmichael@capa.com

Click here to learn how patronMAIL can power your email campaigns

If you would like to forward this e-mail to a friend or colleague, click here.
To be removed from future mailings, reply with REMOVE in the subject line or click here.
If you would like to change your e-mail preferences or update your e-mail address, click here.

Fourplay image used courtesy of Artista Associated Labels, a unit of BMG music.

I recommend that every institution publish a monthly e-mail newsletter that is sent to everyone on their list. Naturally, there can be many editions of the newsletter targeted by interest, or by category (subscribers vs. non-subscribers) but everyone should be reached each month, whether or not your organization is "in season" or not. These mailings are typically filled with information designed to educate, reinforce and promote the institution, its activities and mission.

The content of the newsletter is a series of very short articles with pictures and links designed to direct traffic from the e-mail newsletter to your Web site.

These short articles – 50 to 100 words at the most—are designed as teasers to direct patrons to your Web site for more information. The simpler and more direct these are, the better they work.

Action Oriented E-Postcard

The main goal here is to motivate an action—a click to a Web site, a sale or some other directed action. The more focused these e-postcards are the better. This typically means less copy than more, and a simple and direct visual approach.

We have found that if you try to have multiple goals in one e-postcard, you'll fail to achieve your main goal. E-postcards should then be used to supplement your e-newsletters, targeting segments of your list with specific offers during the month.

Here's an example of a targeted e-postcard designed to motivate the purchase of discounted tickets to see an Off-Broadway show in New York City:

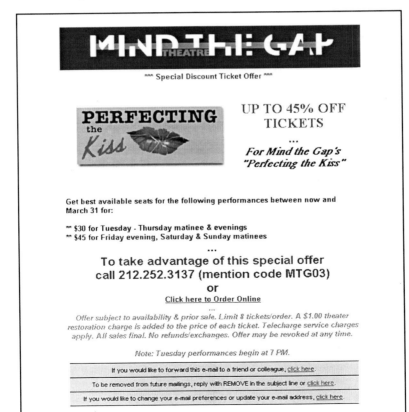

There's a real art to subject lines, and you'll only know what works after you test repeatedly with your own audience, and measure your response rates. That said, here are some general rules to follow:

- Identify yourself – make sure your "brand" or organization name is unmistakable.
- Make the purpose clear: "Santa Fe Quartet – Feb. 2002 Newsletter" is better than "Good News – Our CD has been released."
- Keep it short – you only have about eight to ten words.
- Make it consistent – if you mail regularly, then use the same format each time, so that your readers will instantly recognize your newsletter.

Here are some examples of subject lines from recent client campaigns:

Symphony Holiday Pops Ticket Offer for You!
Limited number of FREE tickets for Chicago City Limits
Eos performs Copland Redux - special Web offer
Spring Programs and Events at the Whitney
Half-Term Photo Fun at the V&A

Finally, at the heart of all e-mail marketing (and frankly all direct marketing) is relevance and value. The bottom line of why e-mail campaigns either fail or don't fail is the offer itself. Your e-mail communications should ideally offer value in one of the following ways:

- More detailed information than is available to the public
- Early notice of events or offers
- Private offers or discounts

E-mail recipients want to feel special – they want something that's not available to the general public. The more you deliver this to them, the more likely it is that they will respond to your communications in the future.

If your message is merely self-promotion that states the obvious, consumers are too smart and they will reject it. Just sending them information by e-mail won't magically change their behavior.

You must deliver value. So don't make the mistake of sending pabulum and expecting stellar results.

CHAPTER 10

Frequently Asked Questions

Why should I do e-mail marketing if we don't have a large list?

Small lists beget big lists, and with the proper effort, your list can grow quickly. Even if you don't have a large list, your patrons are already getting e-mail from other arts organizations, and you're missing an opportunity.

If you believe, as I do, that every organization will be doing some form of e-mail marketing in the years to come, the sooner you get started the better. Even a mailing of 500 messages per month is better than doing nothing at all.

Why can't I do e-mail marketing with Microsoft Outlook?

Microsoft Outlook was designed for personal one-to-one e-mail mailings. Though you can paste 500 names in the "To:" field, you cannot do any of the other things outlined in my "Smart Tips" section. Most importantly, you can't track response rates, which defeats the entire purpose of this kind of marketing.

Just as you would not use the Xerox copier to print your season brochure, don't think about cutting corners on e-mail marketing.

What kind of software should I use?

This is an area in which I am admittedly biased. The company I founded and run, Patron Technology, offers PatronMail—a low-cost e-mail marketing system that handles all the things we've discussed above and more.

Needless to say, I think it's the very best software for arts organizations, as it was developed by people who have worked extensively in the arts industry.

There are certainly other options, some significantly more expensive and others less expensive, but ours is the only one that's been developed by people who understand the unique challenges facing arts marketing directors first-hand.

With over 90 clients in the U.S. and the U.K., we're specialists, and as such we provide our clients with information based on the collective experience of our entire client base.

Not only that, PatronMail is affordable. Many organizations pay as little as $100 per month. That's the end of my advertisement. You can see more at www.patrontechnology.com.

What's the value of a privacy policy and what should it say?

All consumer Web sites ought to have a section available from every page of their site that spells out the agreement between the site and the user with respect to information provided by the user.

This is commonly known as a privacy policy, whose purpose is to assure consumers that you will only use their private information in the ways you inform them.

Most privacy policies explicitly state that the site won't sell, trade or in any other way share information that is collected. For an example of a privacy policy, look at www.patrontechnology.com/privacy.cfm.

Do I need to have HTML skills?

No. If you use proper professional e-mail marketing software, you do not need to have any technical skills beyond what you might use in creating a simple Microsoft Word document.

In what department do our e-mail efforts belong?

Marketing. Unfortunately, because e-mail and Web sites have something to do with technology, many managers think that the strategy and execution of them belongs with the technology deparment.

This is just plain wrong.

My recommendation is that the marketing department should control online marketing. After all, it *is* marketing, delivered electronically.

What if we don't offer online purchasing yet?

Though e-mail marketing can motivate online transactions well, nothing says that you need to offer online transactions to do e-mail marketing. Regular contact from your organization will improve awareness of your audience, even if you can't provide a way for them to buy online yet.

If you're considering adding online transaction capability, many organizations use third parties such as Ticketmaster, Tickets.com and Telecharge to handle their online transactions. That way, since you already have an e-mail mailing list, all you need do is place a "buy here" link directly to those online selling sites to handle your transactions from within your newsletter.

If e-mail is so successful, should I stop doing direct mail?

Not yet. E-mail marketing should first become an integral part of your overall marketing mix, used along with the other formats you currently use.

Although many e-mail recipients say they prefer e-mail over direct mail, I think the combined effect of many types of messages in many formats is the smartest kind of marketing today.

Most likely you will shift costs from one type of marketing to another, and cut back on print in favor of e-mail, as you get more comfortable with the kinds of responses you're getting from e-mail.

What if I don't have the budget for e-mail marketing?

If you have a marketing budget at all, you have money for e-mail marketing. If you are experiencing very tight or diminishing budgets I urge you to enforce a highly rigorous return on investment analysis on your existing marketing techniques.

Figure out how much it costs you to acquire a new customer, to renew a patron, or to subscribe someone. Then apply the costs of the media against the revenue it is bringing in.

If you can't track it, I dare say you shouldn't do it. There are lots of ways to track results, even after the fact. Don't let an inability to track results lull you into a false sense of comfort about how well your current marketing is performing.

My guess is that you'll quickly find that e-mail marketing more than pays for itself. So you do have money for e-mail marketing after all.

What do I need to know about ISPs and Spam?

This could be the subject of an entire book! What you need to understand is that most Internet Service Providers (ISPs) are fighting Spam every day. They typically employ sophisticated software that automatically blocks e-mail that they believe could be Spam. AOL's number one customer complaint is Spam, and as such, AOL blocks more than 750 million messages each day.[38]

Unfortunately, a lot of perfectly acceptable mail from organizations like yours gets blocked because ISP Spam-blockers detect hundreds of e-mails from a single location and quarantine that e-mail, and sometimes don't deliver it at all. A recent study suggested that one in six corporate e-mail messages never gets delivered.[39]

Companies such as ours have "white label" relationships with ISPs. This means that the mail that gets sent from our servers on behalf of our clients is "officially sanctioned" and not subject to Spam-filters.

Spam is an industry-wide problem, and likely to get worse before it gets better. So, as e-mail marketing gets more sophisticated, this is yet another reason why you'll need to employ a professional tool to do it properly.

CHAPTER 11

Final Thoughts

Back in 1995, when I started calling arts organizations asking them to send their season brochures so we could publish their information on a national arts Web site to be known as CultureFinder.com, the reaction from arts marketing executives varied from curious, to enthusiastic, to angry.

I won't recount the number of people who hung up the phone saying "don't bother me with this new technology, I don't have time to do my business as it is, much less take the time to add something new."

Yet only a few years later virtually every arts organization has a Web site. Big or small, updated or outdated, Web sites are *de rigueur*.

So, here I am again extolling the benefits of yet another new marketing scheme—e-mail marketing.

Today, only a fraction of arts organizations take this form of marketing seriously. But, by 2005, I expect virtually all arts organizations to be doing some type of e-mail marketing.

It is my hope that this book has helped you get your arms around this new and revolutionary medium. I further hope that I've helped you understand exactly how enormous the potential is for this new marketing tool, and how you can get started revolutionizing your marketing efforts today with e-mail.

Please don't hesitate to contact me if you'd like more information. I'm one of those people that's online all the time, and I can be reached at gene@patrontechnology.com.

Glossary

Click-through Rate: This is the number of clicks to a specific link within an e-mail. If you send out 10,000 e-mail messages and get 1,200 clicks on a particular link, your Click-through Rate for that link would be 12%.

    The average Click-through Rate for all PatronMail organizations is 4.8%.

HTML: These letters refer to "Hyper Text Markup Language," which is the name of the computer language used to create Web sites and e-mail newsletters that contain graphics and pictures.

Open Rate: The open rate refers to the percentage of patrons who receive an e-mail and/or view it. Imagine being able to be in someone's kitchen when they are opening their regular mail and being able to peek over their shoulder to see which gets their attention, and which they toss into the garbage.

    With e-mail, proper software can track the percentage of patrons that opened a particular e-mail campaign. For example: if you send an e-mail to a list of 1,000 patrons, and 400 of them actually open the e-mail, the Open Rate would be 40%.

    Open Rates are a measure of the interest level your audience has in your mailings. The range of Open Rates for all PatronMail clients in the second half of 2002 was about 30%. The highest Open Rate was 70% and the lowest was 13%.

Unique Patron Clicks: This reflects the number of patrons that click on one or more links within your mailing.

For example, if, of the 400 e-mails that were opened in the previous example, 100 people actually click on a link (or several links) in the e-mail, then the number of Unique Patron Clicks would be 100.

Endnotes

1. EMarketer, January 2003; US Census Bureau, 2002
2. Jupiter Internet Population Model, US Only, April 2000
3. Cellular Telecommunications & Internet Association, 2003
4. The CableCenter, 2003
5. Jupiter Population Model, April 2000
6. InsightExpress, 2002
7. Jupiter Media Metrix, 2002
8. GartnerG2 June, 2001
9. Pew Internet and American Life Project, July 2002
10. Nielsen/NetRating, September 2002
11. Jupiter Internet Shopping Model (US Only), June 2001
    Note: Excluded Travel, Prescription Drugs and Auto
12. Goldman Sachs, Harris Interactive, Nielsen/NetRatings eSpending Report, 2003
13. Neilsen/Netrating March 2003
14. US Census 2000
15. CultureFinder.com Subscriber Survey, 2002
16. CultureFinder National Research Study, 1999
17. CultureFinder.com Subscriber Survey, 2002
18. ibid.
19. ibid.
20. ibid.
21. ibid.
22. ibid.
23. ibid.
24. U.S. Post Office Annual Report, 2002
25. eMarketer, 2001
26. CultureFinder.com Subscriber Survey, 2002
27. ibid.
28. ibid.
29. USA Today- *BrightMail*, 2003
30. CultureFinder.com Subscriber Survey, 2002
31. ibid.
32. ibid.
33. ibid.
34. Return Path, March 2003
35. DoubleClick Q4 2002 Email Trend Report, March 2003
36. ibid.
37. ibid.
38. DoubleClick Smart Marketing Report, March 2003
39. Assurance Systems, 2003